CELEBRATING DIFFERENT BELIEFS

By Steffi Cavell-Clarke

Our
Values

©This edition was
published in 2018.
First published in 2017.

Book Life
King's Lynn
Norfolk PE30 4LS

ISBN: 978-1-78637-112-6

Written by:
Steffi Cavell-Clarke

Edited by:
Grace Jones

Designed by:
Natalie Carr

A catalogue record for this book
is available from the British Library.

CONTENTS

Words that look like **this** can be found in the glossary on page 24.

WHAT ARE OUR VALUES?

Values are ideas and beliefs that help us to work and live together in a **community**. Values teach us how to behave and how to **respect** each other and ourselves.

Respecting others

Understanding different faiths

Making your own choices

Being responsible

Our Values

Helping others

Sharing your ideas

Respecting the law

Listening to others

5

WHAT IS RELIGION?

To follow a religion is to is to **worship** and believe in something, usually a god or gods. Many religions have important places of worship, certain **traditions** and often celebrate special occasions called festivals.

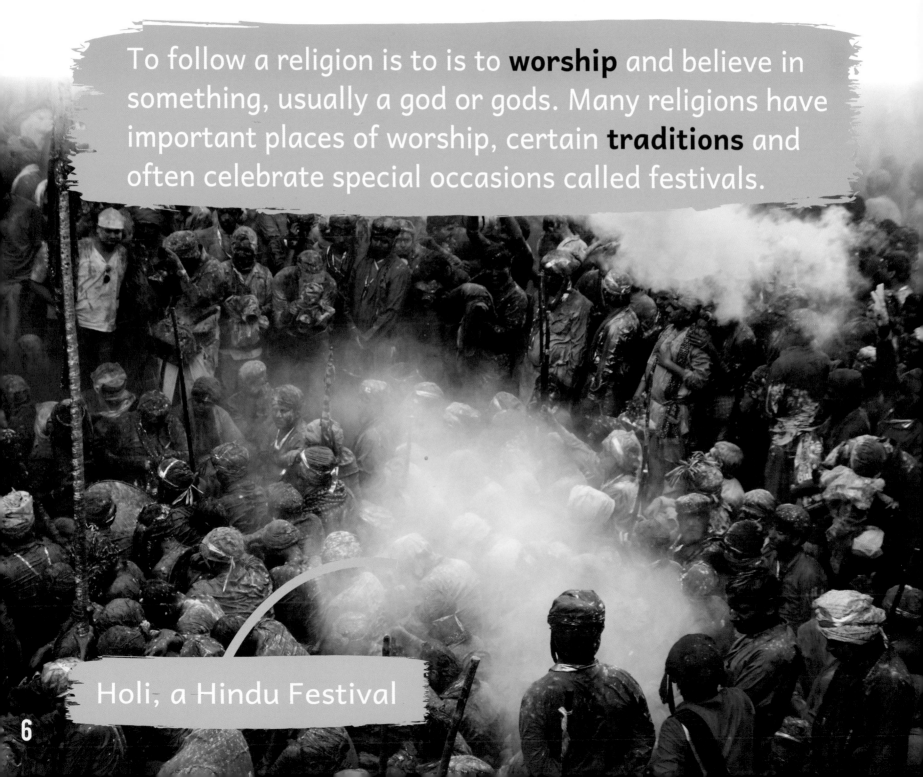

Holi, a Hindu Festival

There are many people who follow a religion, but there are also people who are not **religious**. We are all equal, no matter what we believe in.

People who do not believe in a god or gods are called atheists.

WHY IS IT IMPORTANT?

Religion can help us to understand and follow values.
It can teach us to be kind and caring towards other people.

It is important to show **tolerance** and acceptance of other beliefs.

It is important to remember that we all have the **freedom** to believe in whatever we choose.

DIFFERENT RELIGIONS

There are many different types of religion that are practised all around the world. Some of the religions with the most followers are Christianity, Islam, Hinduism and Judaism.

I am a Hindu

I am a Christian

I am Muslim

I am Jewish

Sarah celebrates Christmas, a Christian festival.

Leigh celebrates Hanukkah, a Jewish festival.

Sarah is Christian and Leigh is Jewish. They both celebrate different religious festivals, but they both spend them with their family members and receive gifts.

LEARNING ABOUT RELIGION

It is important that we respect other people's religion. One of the ways we can do this is by learning about and understanding other religions.

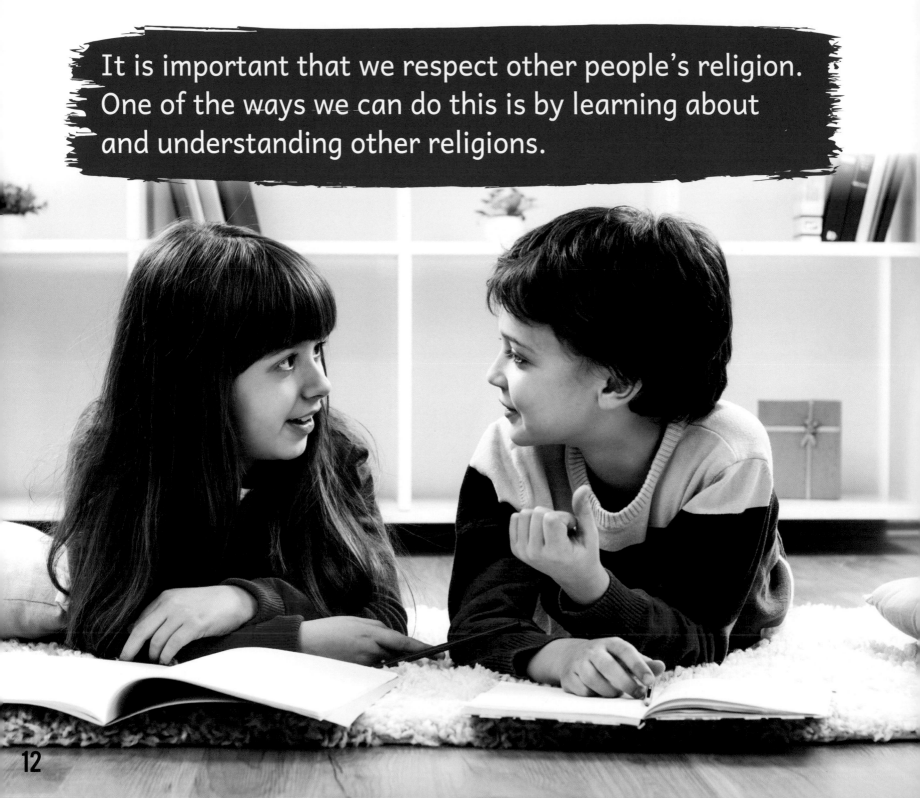

We can learn about religion by asking questions. Sasha asks her dad about Hindu gods and goddesses.

"Hindus believe that the Hindu God, Brahman, is everywhere. He is even a part of us."

SHARING BELIEFS

Sharing our beliefs is an important part of our freedom. We have the right to express ourselves and to practise our religion whenever we choose.

One of the ways that Hindus express their beliefs is at a special festival called Holi. Holi is a spring festival and is celebrated with singing, dancing and by throwing bright and colourful powder at one another.

LISTENING TO OTHERS

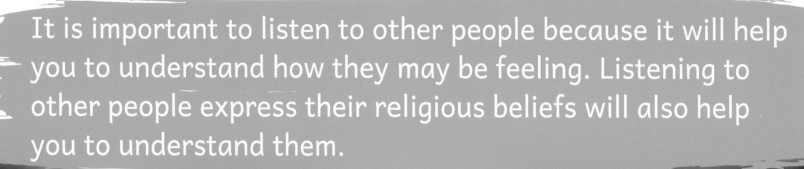

It is important to listen to other people because it will help you to understand how they may be feeling. Listening to other people express their religious beliefs will also help you to understand them.

Marya's classmates wondered why Marya wore a headscarf to school. They listened to Marya as she explained why she wears a special headscarf called a hijab.

"I wear a hijab as a sign of respect to God."

CELEBRATING BELIEFS AT SCHOOL

At school we can learn all about different religions. If we ever have a question about another religion, we can always ask our teacher.

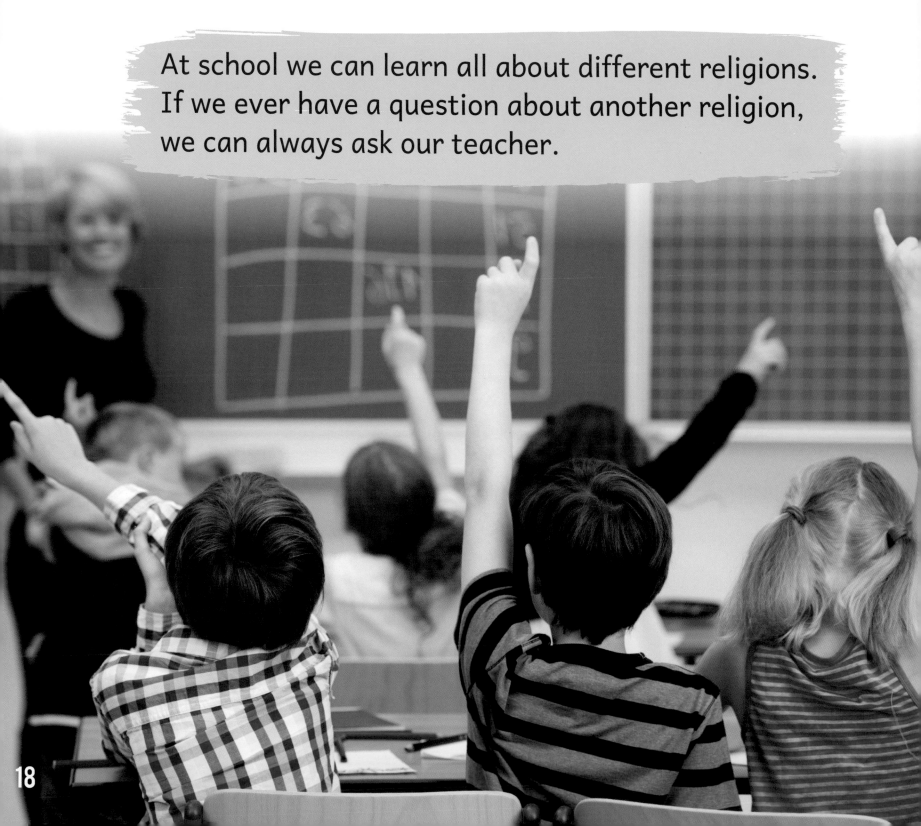

It is important that we respect other people's beliefs at school.

Sasha doesn't celebrate the Christian festival of Easter, but she made a card for her friend who does to help her celebrate and to show her that she cares.

CELEBRATING BELIEFS AT HOME

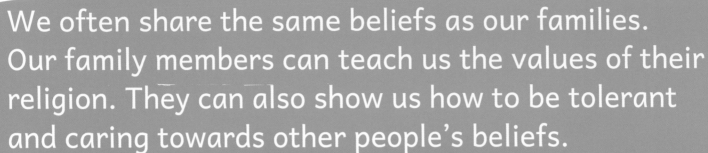

We often share the same beliefs as our families. Our family members can teach us the values of their religion. They can also show us how to be tolerant and caring towards other people's beliefs.

Leigh celebrates the Jewish festival Hanukkah with her family. They sing songs and light special candles on a menorah. This makes Leigh feel close to her family members as they celebrate together.

Menorah

MAKING A DIFFERENCE

You can make a difference by simply learning about other religions. It will help you to be respectful and understanding towards those who have different beliefs to your own.

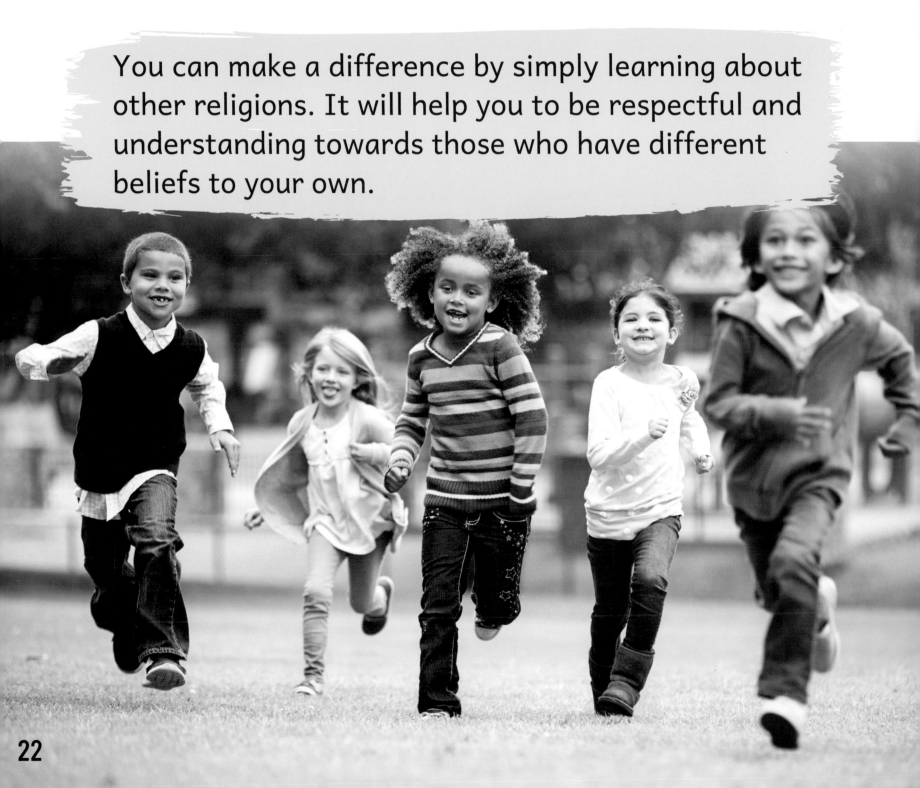

Choose a religion and try to find the answers to these questions:

1. What do they believe?

2. Where is their place of worship?

3. Do they have any special festivals?

4. Do they wear any special clothes?

5. Do they eat any special foods?

23

GLOSSARY

community	a group of people living in the same area who share the same values
freedom	being allowed to do something
law	rules that a community has to follow
religious	following a religion
respect	feeling that something or someone is important
responsible	to be trusted to do the right thing
tolerance	accepting opinions and beliefs that are different from our own
traditions	ways of behaving that have been done over a long time
worship	to show a feeling of respect towards a god or gods

INDEX

PHOTO CREDITS

Photocredits: Abbreviations: l–left, r –right, b –bottom, t –top, c-centre, m –middle.
Front Cover – Bosnian. 2-3 – Ruslan Guzov. 4 – Rawpixel.com. 5tl – Monkey Business Images. 5tm – Tom Wang. 5tr – Yuliya Evstratenko. 5ml – Andresr. 5mr – ISchmidt. 5bl – Lucian Milasan. 5bm – Pressmaster. 5br – Luis Molinero. 6 - AJP. 7 - Rawpixel.com. 8 - Edward Lara. 9 - Bosnian. 10br - szefei. 10bm - natushm. 10ml - YanLev. 10mr - ZouZou. 11l - Ulza. 11r - Noam Armonn. 12 - InesBazdar. 13 - szefei. 14 - wavebreakmedia. 15 - AJP. 16 - Pressmaster. 17 - Hasnuddin. 18 - racorn. 19 - Sergey Nivens. 20 - szefei. 21 - Noam Armonn. 22 - Monkey Business Images. 23 - szefei.
Images are courtesy of Shutterstock.com. With thanks to Getty Images, Thinkstock Photo and iStockphoto.